LIBYA

A CIVILIZATION AMIDST THE DUNES

WHITE STAR PUBLISHERS

Texts
Giorgio Galanti

Contents

1 This relief, dating back to the Roman era and conserved at the Museum of Bani Walid, portrays a date gatherer in the process of climbing a palm tree to reach its fruit.

2-3 The rocky sandstone formations in the area of Akakus, in the extreme southwest of the Libyan Sahara, are the result of an erosive phenomenon. Spires, arches, upside-down pyramids, and a thousand other shapes taken on by the sandstone communicate with the shifting softness of the fine sand dunes. The overall effect is a constant play of light and shadow, of openings and closings.

4-5 Apollonia, outlet to the sea and the main commercial port of Cyrene during the period of Roman and Greek domination, has today partially slipped into the cobalt blue of the Cyrenaic Sea. The rising of the waters has covered the oldest areas.

The Byzantine part, with its splendid basilicas, forms the new shoreline of this place that runs for about a half-mile, caressed by the sound of the waves, poised between the past and the present.

6 The typical Tuareg head covering, usually black and white, takes on the gaudy colors required on the most important Islamic holiday, Aid el-Kebir. The gaze belongs to one of those proud people who, in spite of not appreciating it, have started to get used to the intrusion of tourists.

7 Umm al-Ma, or the "mother of the waters," is the long and narrow reservoir that glistens like a long snake between the dunes of the Ramla Douada, the sandy desert west of Sebha, the capital of Fezzan. The reflections of palm, tamarisk, and eucalyptus trees color the lake, in turn coloring themselves in its silvery highlights.

© 2004 White Star s.p.a.
Via C. Sassone, 22/24
13100 Vercelli, Italy
www.whitestar.it

TRANSLATION
Amy Christine Ezrin

ISBN 13: 978-88-544-0260-7

REPRINTS:
2 3 4 5 6   11 10 09 08 07

Printed in Singapore
Color separation: Fotomec, Turin

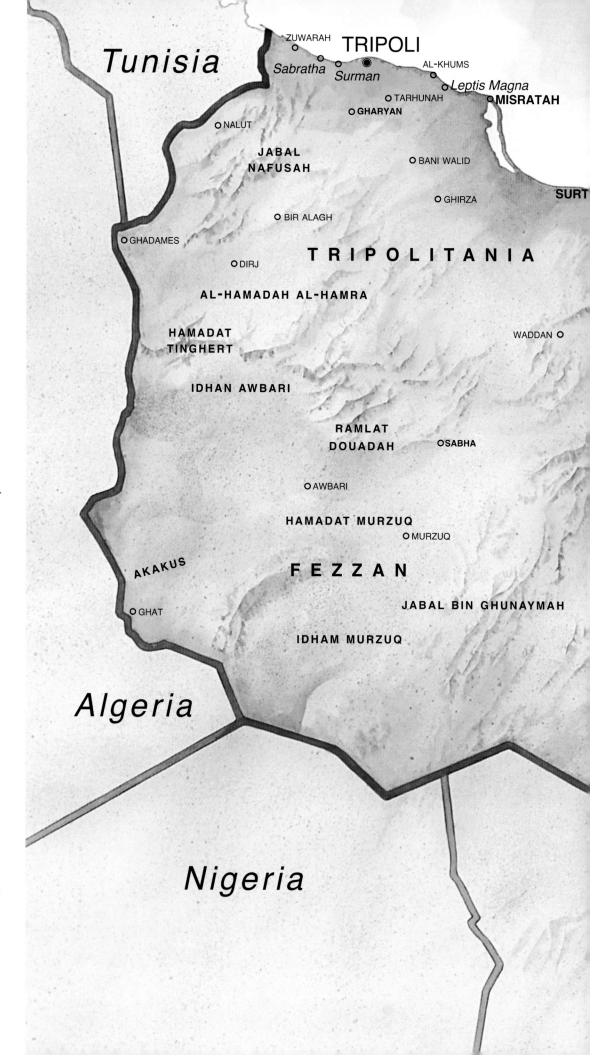

10-11 *October is the month in which the dates reach maturity and their sweet energy spreads throughout the country. During this period, Ghadames holds a festival, which year after year becomes ever more elaborate and popular. Even children take part with the enthusiasm, happiness, and gentleness these desert people demonstrate.*

12-13 *The well-restored decorations give a good idea of the atmosphere in which the inhabitants of Ghadames have lived for centuries. Houses restored to their original splendor by their long-time owners are ever more numerous. Shown here is the central room where guests are received, where the worlds of men and women meet, and where, today, it is possible to savor an excellent plate of couscous while sitting on opulent handmade carpets.*

14-15 *In the area of East Tripoli, a ship is departing for Malta from the modern structure of the tourist port. Connections are frequent with the Mediterranean island, a bridge to the rest of Europe. Just above the port, the white dome and minaret of a recently built mosque stand out. White is the dominant color of religious buildings, with the exception of the city's main mosque, the Pink Mosque.*

Mediterranean Sea

Ptolemais *Cyrene* *Apollonia*
TUKRAH AL-BAIDA **DERNA** *Gulf of Bumbah*

BENGHAZI **TUBRUK**

Gulf of Sidra **AL-JABAL AL-AKHDAR** AL-BURDI

AJDABIYA **M A R M A R I C A**

MARSA AL-BURAYQAH

AL-JAGHBUB

Oases of Djaluh **Egypt**

C Y R E N A I C A

SARIR

BAHR AR-RIMAL AL-AZIM

BAHR AR-RAMLA AL-KABIR

ZIGHAN

RAMLAT RABYANAH **L I B Y A N
D E S E R T**

AL-KUFRAH

AL-UWAYNAT

Chad *Sudan*

Introduction

Libya, hidden from the eyes of Wester,3n tourists until recently, has opened its borders, making its inestimable environmental and archeological treasures available to all. Visiting the country means entering into a prehistoric world of rock drawings with unexpected archeological riches, a world of a thousand deserts with blue lakes and white oases, and a world of colonial architecture with strong traditional connotations. However, it also means encountering a modern world that moves ahead among satellite dishes, the latest models produced by planetary technology and the most advanced form of communication.

Libya's shore boasts more than 1,200 miles of Mediterranean coastline, stretching from the western border of Tunisia to the opposite border shared with Egypt, at the easternmost point of the country. On the south coast of this open, vast sea, the view extends as far as the horizon without ever encountering obstacles, except for the only two tiny little islands in all the country's territory: Farwah, near Tunisia, a sandy tongue with some palm trees, and Bomba, a Cyrenaic reef that has risen to the surface of the sea. The Tripolitan coast is composed of sandstone, where rocks made by the oxidation of the sand have formed steps that descend towards the water. In some points, it is possible to walk along the last of these steps just where the waves break, while in others the bright blue usurps the indentations to create bays of an absolute beauty where the sand, in shades varying from white to ochre, encounters the soft foam at the water's edge.

The area of Psis, about an hour east of Tripoli, which features the beaches around Sabratha, is enchanting for a good part of the year, as long as one stays a proper distance away from the populated areas. The unfortunate habit of discarding refuse near the water has given rise to a nearly continuous garbage dump between the village and the coastline, where scraps mix with rusty cans and bits of indestructible plastic. Fortunately, the settlements are so few in number that, shaded by the eucalyptus trees that grow almost up to the sea, the coast has remained both intact and rolling and wild – the most pristine in all the Mediterranean.

At the middle of the Libyan coast, a recess, from which Sicily appears to have detached in the remote past, forms a wide gulf where the desert meets the sea. This is the region of the Syrtis, the terrible quicksands mentioned by Greek sailors. Here, the mires of water and sand represented constant danger for ships. This area, not suited to swimming precisely because of its ability to deceive, is a unique land and water habitat, the ideal environment for marine life as well as land animals and birds. The chosen spot of sea turtles to deposit their eggs and of numerous bird species that come for the abundant food supply, the Syrtis remains the wildest and least-known area of the country. Its present-day leader comes from this region where, for many years, the Bedouins have lived with their back to the sea, looking after their camel herds or their flocks, the only significant resource available.

The sea of Cyrenaica may be the least alluring and with beaches fewer in number, but in some tracts, the rock that descends directly into the sea exerts a strong appeal, creating a powerful setting. The colors intensify and mix with the green of the dense vegetation of the mountain on which the ancient Greek colonists from Thera decided to found Cyrene. In the past, the entire Libyan coast lived a more intense existence. The underwater ruins are numerous, in addition to those of the many mansions belonging to the rich merchants of Leptis Magna, Cyrene, and Sabratha. Today, far from those historic days, the Libyan sea, plied by the rare fishing boat, speaks of horizons, immense spaces, and the infinite.

Nestled between the slopes of Jebel Nafusa, encircling the Tripolitan coast like a crown, extend the most significant Libyan plains: the Jifarah, an Arab term indicating any flat zone whatsoever, refers to the plains of Tripolitania, the flatlands *par excellence,* in a territory that is 90 percent desert. It is crossed by descending towards Tripoli from Tunisia, or vice versa. Before the Italian occupation, thousands of wells provided fresh water to irrigate the palm groves, the main crop at the time. The arrival of the Italians, who brought with them thousands of farmer-colonists from the mother country, contributed to the development of agriculture. The territory was divided into lots called "grants," and the new property owners gave a fresh boost to farming activities by expanding the cultivated zones, introducing new species, and more intensively exploiting existent practices.

Today, despite the fact that many farms sit in a state of abandon, traveling the coastal Tripolitan road means being swallowed up into the shade and unmistakable scent of long rows of eucalyptus trees. Thanks to the growth of their foliage, they shade vast areas and protect them from the strong wind, while their roots assure solidity to the land, thus deterring the build-up of troublesome sand dunes in the inhabited areas.

In some zones, excellent citrus fruits are produced, above all oranges and lemons, which are then sold, freshly picked, in the markets that skirt the main roads. Reaching towards the sky, palms with long trunks wave their fronds, sometimes alongside stark cypress trees bordering the driveways to the farms. Cluster pines complete the Mediterranean scene of these green plains, squeezed between the sea and the heights of Jebel Nafusa, affording surprising Italian-like vistas.

In the other Libya, that of the Cyrenaica, almost another country compared to that of the Tripoli area, rise the peaks of the Green Mountain, Jebel al-Akhdar. Green thanks to the abundance of water from the sky and underground sources that supply this fortunate region, it was settled as early as the days of Ancient Greece. Impressive archeological remains sit comfortably atop one of the vast natural terraces overlooking the

16 top The leader, Mohammar Gheddafi, towers over every part of the country: the posters portraying him in an infinite number of poses and situations are designed and produced within the university's Fine Arts department, and they represent the most explicit and also iconic artistic element found in the desert enveloping Libya.

16 bottom Dozens of masterpieces, salvaged during the excavations at Leptis Magna, have been placed in the small but full museum standing next to the archeological area.

17 top Tuareg dances, in which only men perform, tell the stories of duels, swords, shields, and clubs, powerful and muscular objects that contrast with the lightness of the steps, the harmony of the movements, and the constant smiles on the faces of the dancers.

17 bottom Female Libyan children have started to abandon the traditional headscarf and dress of their mothers, preferring more and more to dress in a more "television"-like style. The profuse number of satellite dishes has brought the outside world into Libyan households with growing frequency.

18-19 The imposing appearance of the temple of Zeus, in the upper part of Cyrene, compensates for all the hard work of the many archeologists who contributed to saving a good part of this magnificent building.

20-21 From the hill on which Cyrene stands, the view extends as far as the sea and reaches, at the edge of the coast, the ancient columns of Apollonia. The road running between the two archeological areas winds through the immense necropolises around Cyrene that occupy the entire surrounding hill.

Mediterranean, blessed by the fresh air found at an altitude of 5,250 feet supplemented by abundant vegetation, where limpid water gushes from springs used since ancient times. The sea and the port of Apollonia are located just a few miles away. The combination can only recall the first Greek colonists that recognized in this place the description given by the god Apollo upon being questioned at Delphi, before their adventurous departure for the Libyan coasts.

The mountain occupies a large part of the peninsula and, in some places, reaches right up to the sea. Higher up, deep gorges gouged by ancient rivers criss-cross the harsh and jagged territory that long hid the hero of the Libyan resistance: Omar al-Mukhtar. Sitting on a rock, between this ancient sea and the Green Mountain, among the columns of Greek temples and cooled by an almost incessant wind, it is not difficult to tune in to the past and feel on one's skin that sun, that salt, and that scent that come from distant times.

The desert is ever-present in Libya; it can be found in any corner of the country. Even in that 10 percent of the territory where the rocks or dunes have not taken over, on the coast or among the mountains of the east or west, the southern wind carries the fine, fine sand. It clouds one's sight, muffling the atmosphere on days of the gibleh, and penetrates everywhere, including the most hermetic hollow spaces into where even a drop of water could not pass – into the pages of a book and into everyone's bodies. The desert advances slowly with its moving dunes that the vegetation seeks with difficulty to contain. It stretches out softly into the sea, as in the region of the Syrtis, or oxidizes into sandstone near the coast. Since time immemorial, the Libyans have grown used to dealing with the desert. Their culture is steeped in the desert, its silences, its expectations, and in the long and tiring crossings in search of a drop of water, of which the end itself recalls the idea of abandon rather than that of absence.

However, in Libya one cannot speak of a single kind of desert. The peoples that have inhabited the country have always used different names to identify the "deserts," just as much farther north, among the populations of the Arctic, the word "snow" is not sufficient to describe the various manifestations of the white cloak. Traveling down to Tripoli towards the Fezzan, the southwest region of the country, and crossing Jebel Nafusa, which reaches an altitude of about 2,600 feet, there is an area of pre-desert. On this expansive plain of hardened sand grows the "esparto" bush, a plant that, in the past, was used to make paper and rope. Rare acacias open their umbrella of leaves under which men, goats, and camels seek shade during the sunniest hours. Slowly, the vegetation grows scarcer as the *hamadah,* the desert of stone composed of great slabs of stratified rock, takes the upper hand.

Beyond the immense expanse of the Hamadah el-Hamra, in the borderlands between Tunisia and Algeria, one of the outstanding pearls of the Libyan desert waits to be discovered: the oasis and city of Ghadames. Today, new buildings surround the old *medina,* where the last remaining inhabitants of the old city went to live during the 1980s.

Ghadames is like one immense building that used to accommodate nearly 8,000 people. It is entered via a few gates that, in the past, were closed at night. Inside, it seems like an alien world. An extremely intricate labyrinth of covered lanes and alleys unravels across the whole city. The intensely blue sky can be only seen by popping out into one of the tiny squares in which, during the sunny days of summer, the elders gather: the Square of the Big Mulberry Tree and the Square of the Little Mulberry Tree. Such naïve place names recall the simplicity of Ghadames' culture.

The dwellings, decorated with great care according to a typical style, are entered by way of the lanes, and a door made of palm wood protects the privacy of each family group. The houses of Ghadames expand vertically around a large central room where guests are received and couscous and tea are shared. In such rooms, the world of women unfolded, occupying the terraces and using passageways that connected all the residences to the world of men, teeming out in the covered alleys.

Dozens of mosques with their tall minarets, Koranic schools, and public buildings are enclosed by and incorporated into the shifting whiteness of the hand-smoothed walls. It is not surprising that old Ghadames is part of the world's heritage, recognized by UNESCO. Exiting the old city and passing through the perfect gardens, where water was distributed among farmers according to a system of absolute equality, is to leave behind the central nucleus of the dream that Libya invites us to experience.

Further south appear the first dunes of the Erg, the sandy deserts known as *ramlah* for their smaller size, which alternate with areas of pebbles mixed with sand called *serir*. West of Sebha, the capital of Fezzan, extend two of the most enchanting sandy areas of the Libyan Sahara. Firstly, the Ramlah Douadah, where the medium-height dunes surround a couple dozen lakes, is a paradise where the air quality, the softness of the shapes in the sand, and the surreal blue of the lakes create a magical setting. Then, the Murzuq Desert, an area rarely visited by the caravans of tourist-explorers, features chains of dunes up to a few hundred feet tall, which define this harsh, savage, and difficult-to-explore territory that is, however, unique among the Libyan "deserts."

Even further southwest, in the heart of the Sahara, the natural sculptures of the Akakus Mountains, the most-traveled zone in all the Libyan desert, sit upon a carpet of sand. Here, the gentleness of the soft sands and the natural rock sculptures that form arches, spires shooting up towards the blue sky, and emergent boulders as if in an immense golden sea combine with the remnants of ancient wall drawings. Hundreds of rocky sites can be discovered by navigating this labyrinth of narrow passages, delicate hollows, and natural amphitheaters where the infrequent camps of tourists cross paths and, sometimes, the caravans of the still-nomadic Tuaregs. Amazingly, after hours or days of traveling, palms swaying in the wind emerge slowly on the horizon. That is how oases appear, mysteriously, the offspring of underground water sources, the geological mysteries of the desert. In fact, in the not so recent past,

the whole area of the Sahara could count on a good distribution of above-ground water sources. Now, the underground streams have disappeared, leaving behind the dry beds of the *wadi*, but their presence is still indicated by vegetation, groups of palm trees, the delicate foliage of tamarisk trees, or the scent of eucalyptus trees that transform the dryness and sunny conditions of the desert into a place for meeting, resting, and living.

In prehistoric times, the Libyan Desert was certainly more populated than it is today. The environment was more favorable and water ran in larger quantities, even on the surface. As a result, many animals provided both a source of food and farm labor for the nomadic and sedentary populations of the time. Numerous remains, often easy to discover in some areas, attest to a large presence of human settlements.

Desertification required that the permanent inhabitants traveled to search for water, pasture land, and trading places. In the area of Fezzan, where the present-day presence of an aquifer several feet underground makes life there still possible, the Garamantes civilization long flourished. This people both encountered and survived the Roman domination of the area. According to the iconography available today, they have been portrayed as and imagined to be highly skilled charioteers driving very lightweight chariots pulled by horses, flying across the dunes that rose next to their capital, Garama, present-day Germa.

The remains of what was once one of the most important cities in the area can still be visited today. Houses, a fortified *kasbah*, intricate alleys, and food storehouses, all molded by the hands of the builders, rise from the ground like earthen sculptures, like works of art that have survived the years, like sculptural creations entangled with the ever-present palm trees. All around the tens of thousands of tombs that constitute the largest necropolis in the country, traces testify to the fact that the "Valley of Life" was also a place of passage for many generations of nomads and, later on, pilgrims on route to Mecca. The desert silence never forgets, and a pile of stones set to indicate a burial place can remain unaltered and immobile for thousands of years.

During the same period, people on the Mediterranean coast lived through different events. The sandstone bays or the landing spots on the Cyrenaic peninsula were used by the earliest, cautious sailors, whether Phoenician or Punic, and simple market towns began to pop up, where goods were exchanged with inland peoples and where sailors could wait out the long winter break. These same market towns then grew to become the first important Punic cities. One of these was Sabratha, the westernmost of three *polis*. The others were Oea (present-day Tripoli) and Leptis Magna, all of which still feature numerous buildings, temples, and mausoleums from that period.

The Greeks to the east and the Romans to the west gave an enormous impetus to life in the coastal cities, which, from a commercial point of view, enjoyed a strategic position as a point of passage for all goods coming out of the depths of Africa, such as ivory,

animals, slaves, and precious stones. Leptis Magna had the honor of being the birthplace of Septimius Severus, who became emperor of Rome, thus beginning the Severus Dynasty. In his honor and thanks to considerable investment, the city of Leptis was completely "marbled." In other words, the main public buildings, temples, and the forum were lined with the most precious kinds of marble imported from Greece, Italy, and even more distant places. The Baths of Hadrian, one of the most amazing places in all the city, shone with the shades of prized marbles and were adorned with hundreds of excellently made statues. Leptis became *magna* thanks to this period of artistic and architectural fervor between the first and third centuries B.C.

As the city began to overcrowd and, more importantly, when its port started to show embarrassing signs of decay owing to the invading sands, the wealthy Leptis merchants moved out along the coast, building marvelous villas, of which the remains of some are still visible. A few miles west of Leptis, the villa Silin is stunning with its decorations and, above all, its mosaic floors. Fortunately, a wise decision on the part of the Libyan Department of Archeology was made to restore and leave on site the villa's valuable collection of mosaics. During tours, caressed by the constant breeze wafting off the sea, visitors remain enchanted by the artistic quality of the numerous mosaics on the floors of the various rooms. The geometric designs, precise and diverse, alternate with illustrations of floral elements, birds, the lovely Lycurgus wrapped in grapevines, and chariot races. Outside the villa, the private baths, the dock, and the kitchens attest to the wealth, self-sufficiency, and opulence of these villas that, inserted into surroundings of rare natural beauty, still excite visitors today.

Beyond the "terrible Syrtis" that terrorized even the most expert helmsmen, a circle of territory outside the Punic influence was able to develop on the Cyrenaic peninsula. This "Greek" zone of Libya grew to become the Pentapolis, a group of cities that interrelated thanks to their strong sense of cultural identity. Touring Cyrene, Tocra, Ptolemais, Apollonia, and Berenice (in the area of present-day Benghazi) is like a voyage through Greek archeology, the Greco-Libyan society, and a fascinating dive into the civilizations to which Ancient Roman culture was enormously beholden.

During the centuries following the collapse of the Roman Empire in the present-day area of Libya, waves of Vandals and Byzantines followed one after the other. The latter left behind the splendid basilicas that were built upon pre-existent buildings, adapting them to their new function and adding a new touch with characteristic mosaics. In the seventh century A.D., the Arab invasion marked the destiny of the whole region, defining what the dominant culture would be for all the centuries to come.

The new inhabitants settled throughout the territory. The Berbers were forced to seek refuge in the difficult-to-reach mountainous regions, and there they continued to live and build the "granary" fortresses that are one of the main attractions of the country's interior. They are closed structures, with a circular or oval layout, where the provisions of the entire village were stored in hundreds of cells within the building. It was a kind of incredible hive where each inhabitant had his own cell, and it was also a place where, when necessary, the population could hide from enemy attacks and survive for long periods by sharing the victuals. Today, in the mountainous region south of Tripoli, some of these splendid examples of collective defense and survival strategy can be visited; Nalut, Kabaw, and Qasr el-Hajj are the most impressive exemplars of this particular type of building.

The successive "bosses" of the Mediterranean would take control of the coastal cities, which remained through the occupier's changing fortunes, until their annexation by the Ottoman Empire. Although belonging to the great empire, the Turks left control of the main cities to some of the local families. One of these was the Karamanli family, which governed Tripolitania for over a century, until 1835.

The Italian colonization began in 1911, clashing with the Turkish forces. It brought great urban and agricultural innovations to the country, along with a form of colonialism similar to that implemented by other European countries in Africa. Following the Second

World War, Libya obtained independence and was governed by King Idriss of the Senussi Dynasty until the 1969 revolution, which brought its present-day leader into power: Mohammar Gheddafi.

In Libya, as in the stricter Islamic countries and according to the dictates of the Koran, an indisputable veto applies to all forms of iconic communication. Images are banned from all public spaces in the cities, with the obvious exception – the exception of exceptions – of the image of Gheddafi, leader of the revolution and of the country for 34 years. His face and body stand out on giant billboards, where he can be recognized in the guise of a firm army colonel, a proud Bedouin wrapped in a long white gown, or a warrior of Islam on horseback with a drawn sword, incinerating hordes of infidels with his stare. Immense pictorial works portray him in infinite poses that watch over – or spy on – his people.

His image looms over the intricate street junctions, above and below ground, which abound in the main cities. In Libya, roads are not lacking. In and out of the city, automobiles speed off in all directions, puffing out from their exhaust pipes the oxides of a substance that costs next to nothing: oil.

24 Rock drawings drew their subjects mostly from the events and rituals of daily life. The drawing, which portrays cattle, belongs to the phase called "pastoral" in Saharan culture.

24-25 The so-called "bogeys" are unidentified animals. The great variety of styles present in the rock drawings has long made it difficult to classify and date them.

25 Giraffes appear on the sandstone walls of Messak, proof of their presence in times when water sources on the ground surface were more abundant than today.

26-27 In the Akakus, erosive phenomena have given rise to natural sculptures such as this enormous arch.

27 The minerals contained in the rocks create unusual colors – strong pastel tints or soft earthy hues.

The discovery of the black gold has contributed more than any other factor to the personality of modern Libya. The big, worldwide industry has brought billions of dollars to the government coffers, taking the form of new residences, schools, giant mosques, roads, and the Big River, a waterworks project that is unique in the world for its scale. From reservoirs of water, discovered more than 3,000 feet underground in the middle of the desert, a system of pumps and wide-diameter conduits (about 13 feet across) carries the precious liquid to the coastal cities where it spreads out through the urban hydraulic network, supplying the population with water.

The new and sudden wealth has afforded unexpected prosperity to a good part of the population that, more in the past than today, has been able to take full advantage of this fortune, often leaving behind handicraft trades or small businesses that were certainly less lucrative. However, the mining of oil and its derivates, sucked up from the depths of the earth, takes a heavy toll on the environment. The country suffers from productive hypertrophy in the sector, and everywhere thousands of plastic bags flutter around, the unchecked use of which

has not been limited by the relatively scarce public education in refuse management. Thousands of automobile, truck, and van carcasses rest alongside every roadway, plastic objects invade beaches, and gasoline fumes from old and poorly maintained motors rise like cries of pain from the cities.

This is a troubling aspect of a country that has become wealthy too quickly and undergone a process of modernization that, when not taken in small, restrained doses, risks being destructive.

However, the Libyan people have maintained, perhaps in an effort to ward off unfamiliar and ambiguous modernity, strong ties to the past, tradition, and their ample assortment of rituals.

Even in Tripoli or Benghazi, which are obviously the places where contacts and closeness with the Western world are more prevalent, the effects of globalization are felt, sparing nothing and no one. Girls can now choose their clothes and often even their husbands and the social and religious ceremonies take opulent, ancient, and detailed forms. They are occasions for meeting,

evaluation, and sometimes confrontation between the large families that constitute the main framework of the Libyan social system.

Weddings, following an exhausting phase of bargaining by the elders of the group, are held according to an established and particular formula. Enormous tents are pitched in the streets, blocking traffic for days at a time if necessary.

Participants will attend either the party for the men or the one for the women, each of which is strictly segragated; they will drink and eat copious amounts to ensure the economic stability of the families; the women will dance until late at night in their fanciest and most modern clothes; and, the young men will demonstrate their abilities as dancers, their social graces, and their discrete submission to the elders in order to obtain their good judgment, which will hopefully provide them with a key to the society of women. That assessment will act as a seal of identification as they make their way through the Libyan world.

Even the final moments of life become a social affair, as the coffins are carried on the shoulders of long convoys of men in white. After the procession, friends and relatives – conveniently fasting – will pay visits to the

28-29 Apollo glows in all of his grace in this sculpture known as "Citaredo." He carries a lyre, which represents his vocation for singing and music. The statue comes from Hadrian's Baths in Leptis Magna and is conserved at the Museum of Tripoli.

29 The Roman replica of the Capitoline Venus, also called "Chastity," dating back to the second century A.D., comes from Hadrian's Baths in Leptis as well and is kept in the rooms of the capital's museum.

30-31 The remaining columns of the ancient theater of Leptis Magna frame the blue of the sea and sky. The building is one of the most magical places in the Roman city. Of course, spectators can no longer see the three orders of overhanging columns on the stage, and the over a hundred statues that adorned it have disappeared, but sitting on the steps of the cavea and letting one's eye wander over the whole city is still an intense experience.

houses of the family in mourning for several days. They will be obliged to come even from far away to bring comfort and to perpetuate the ancient custom.

The main collective ritual that involves the entire Islamic world, despite acquiring different manifestations and nuances in the various countries, is the observation of a month of fasting, otherwise known as Ramadan.

In Libya, this tradition is strictly observed. Being caught chewing anything or even drinking water during the day becomes offensive to whoever practices the fast.

Nobody anywhere in the country will light a cigarette, not even the most desperate addicts. Nobody will sip any liquid, and because the month of fasting follows the Islamic calendar and therefore falls ten more days behind the Western calendar every year, the holiday can occur even during the hottest summer months, when not drinking can be particularly taxing.

After the call of the *muezzin*, who declares the end of the day, abstention from any form of ingestion and sexual relations transforms into a gastronomic feast. The most delicious delicacies of traditional Libyan cuisine appear on the table, every evening for the whole month.

Following dinner, people go out into the city and meet with friends. Flocks of little ones surround their mothers and fathers like chicks as they enjoy the big party. The squares are lit up until late at night, cars drive non-stop around the streets of the towns, and the bars offer drinks (strictly non-alcoholic) and the large *narghileh* for men to smoke.

Finally, around dawn, before the *muezzin* calls to return to the fast, the last meal is consumed, a small energy boost to help people get through another day of Ramadan.

The majority of Libyan cities have grown around a historical center, the old *medina*, which means "city" in Arabic. Inside these dense build-ups of alleys, people, shops, smells, and sounds, numerous *souqs*, or markets, are found within every old city.

Many of them have maintained their ancient vocation and structure. Often covered, they offer clothes, spices, and gold. The gold *souq* in Tripoli is emblematic of a culture that regulates, mitigates, and encourages relationships via the noble metal. Each little boutique is always busy; women especially love the golden pendants for their indisputable beauty and value, but also because they contribute to the establishment of status with the social hierarchy.

As evening falls, when the natural light begins to fade, the windows of the goldsmiths light up, making the necklaces, bracelets, rings, and earrings sparkle. Meanwhile, the *muezzin* makes the call to prayer and the sweet aroma of incense spreads through the air.

Strolling along the peaceful lanes of the *medina*, the preciousness and tenderness of this Islamic-Arab culture, all too often defamed and slighted in recent times because of phenomena alien to its open and tolerant roots, becomes apparent in the Libya of today.

Medinas and Reinforced Concrete

32 top Red Castle, so-called for the color its stones take on when the setting sun lights it from the side, has always been the city's symbol. The building, witness to the long line of changing dynasties in control of Tripoli and enveloped in infamy for having been a site where terribly savage murders were perpetrated, today appears far from those times and smiles slyly in the eyes of new and more peaceful visitors.

32 bottom The medina, crowded with people, scents, and sounds, opens itself up during the day to visits, strolls, and shopping for gold, medicinal herbs, and valuable fabrics. It is a place to be discovered bit by bit. Many of its numerous mosques are hidden among the houses, whereas the ancient caravanserais have been transformed into workshops for new artisans; after a long sleep, old Tripoli is waking up again.

33 Here and there, palm trees that have survived the savage felling of their peers remember that the oasis of Tripoli was once one of the vastest in all of Libya. However, the construction of new neighborhoods outside the medina and then the subsequent expansion of the modern city gutted the immense oasis that, today, winks from the tufts of the palms encircled by the walls of new houses.

Tripoli: A Capital between the Present and the Future

34 top Inside the castle, quarters intended for the residences of the Pasha and his family were built largely during the rule of the Caramanli family, in the 18th and 19th centuries. The patio was one of the unavoidable features of such buildings, and water, which ran down the marble fountains, could not be lacking.

34 center A large door bearing words written in Arabic heralds the entrance to the Museum of the Jamahiriya, the most extensive in all the country. The placement of the artifacts follows a chronological order: from prehistoric origins represented by fossils finds, among which there is a splendid petrified tree, until the contemporary period of the 1969 Revolution.

34 bottom Inside the medina, one of the most important arches built in the Roman period, that of Marcus Aurelius, has miraculously survived. It owes its rescue to the efforts of archeologists. In fact, until the beginning of the twentieth century, it remained half-buried and, incredibly, a space was hollowed out inside it for the projection of early black-and-white films.

35 At night, especially in summer, the Green Square fills with passers-by and cars. The big space, created through the destruction of numerous colonial buildings, is as bright as day thanks to powerful reflectors, as dozens of taxis crowd in, whizzing closely by the patrons of the cafés who come to cool down at the outdoor tables.

36-37 Built in the 1930s and designed by the architect Saul Meraviglia Mantegazza in an intriguing architectural style featuring Arab forms, called "arabisance," the Governor's Palace stands in the center of Tripoli. Today it is called the "Palace of the People," and cultural performances are often held there.

37 top Over the years of the Italian presence in the country, the savings of colonists flowed copiously through the vaults of the Cassa di Risparmio della Libya (Libya Savings and Loan), today the Central Bank of Libya. The building stands out, because of its ochre color, from the dominant whiteness around it and is distinguished by its majestic façade.

37 center Called the "candy box" for its stuccoes and white, finely-wrought decorations, the Gallery De Bono was the hub of colonial-era "highlife." The high society met here during their evening walks and organized their outings to the Miramare Theater or the casino of the Waddan Hotel while sipping coffee at the tables outside the cafés.

37 bottom Only in recent years has Villa Volpi, which belonged to one of the more well-known Italian families to set up residence in Libya, opened its doors to the public. Its park has been converted into a lovely open-air café serving strictly non-alcoholic drinks, coffee, and Libyan tea. Inside, the building contains a small museum.

38-39 The sound of the "beaters" shaping copper grows louder as one approaches the medina. The close quarters of their shops are overflowing with all kinds of objects, among which are decorative spikes with the crescent moon, an important Islamic symbol.

39 top left In the medina, numerous souqs, or markets, are encountered. They are distinguished by the type of goods they sell or the origin of their ancient merchants: the spice souq, the goldsmith's souq, and even the Turkish souq or the Maltese souq.

39 top right The white arches of the medina connect and reinforce the buildings they come into contact with and add that constant touch of roundness typical of Islamic architecture.

39 center Some buildings, such as that shown here, called zawia contain a mosque and areas where students from far away who came to study the Koran once lodged.

39 bottom left The English Consulate is today a small museum, open every day except for Friday. It has been carefully renovated down to the smallest details, including its garments, arms, and everyday objects.

39 bottom right A committee for the artistic preservation of the medina of Tripoli works to bring part of the city back to health. A few buildings have been restored to their original state; others are still in the process of being saved.

40-41 *Right in the middle of the* medina, *around the corner from the intersection of the "four columns" that indicate the heart of the old city, one of the residences of the Caramanli family, lords of Tripoli for over a hundred years, has been converted into a museum. In its numerous rooms, the successful reconstruction of the 18th-to-19th-century spaces can be admired.*

41 top Looking up a bit while walking the narrow streets of the medina *is all it takes to catch glimpses of the spires of the minarets and the crenellation of the towers sprouting from low buildings in the direction of an almost perpetually blue sky. The vast and clear sky drapes over the city like the cloak of a prince.*

41 center The caravanserai were hotels for merchants, with large spaces to store goods and stalls for the animals. They numbered more than 35 before Tripoli grew beyond the limits of the medina. *Long abandoned, today they are being restored, and their old rooms are becoming shops where artisans and shopkeepers can display their merchandise.*

41 bottom Around the corner from the arch of Marcus Aurelius, the most lavish mosque of the medina *of Tripoli is found: the Gurgi Mosque. The excellent artisans that came from Morocco were responsible for the latest redecoration of the building.*

42 Ghirza, about two hours south of Misurata, is a site of great historical and artistic value. Among its characteristic buildings, the ancient mausoleums stand out, tombs for the wealthy of the era. One of these, dismantled and then rebuilt, makes for an impressive exhibit at the Museum of Tripoli.

43 left The photograph shows one of the many statues found at Hadrian's Baths in Leptis Magna, later reunited in the Museum of the Castle. The wealthy of Leptis often commissioned works of art reproducing Greek models from the best sculptors in the Mediterranean.

43 top right The rooms at the entrance of the museum lie outside of the otherwise chronological route that unravels further ahead, and the Capitoline Venus seems to observe the funereal mausoleum of Ghirza with arrogance.

43 bottom right In one of the first rooms of the museum is located the Volkswagen Bug that belonged to the leader Mohammar Gheddafi, before he took part in the revolution that led to a change in the country's look and leaders.

44 left The emperor Marcus Aurelius, portrayed in this statue, wears the lorica, a breastplate that covered the chest and abdomen, yet this one is extremely sophisticated with its fine decorations.

44 center One of the most impressive monuments in Leptis Magna was, and is still today, the arch of Septimius Severus. Risen to the highest imperial offices, this citizen of Leptis had the monument erected at the entrance to the city. Part of the decorative device is found in the Museum of Tripoli.

44 right Athena imperiously dominates one of the rooms of the Tripoli museum from above, thanks to her remarkable size. However, about 2,000 years ago, she dominated the stage of the theater of Leptis Magna with the same proud bearing.

45 In this Roman copy of the Ephesus Artemis, the goddess of the hunt is portrayed in a fascinating version in which, through lovely decorations, her role as protector of fertility, women, and newborns is underlined.

46 *The use of tiny* tesserae *has made it possible to achieve sophisticated color effects in this mosaic from the villa of Tajura, which portrays the face of the god of the sea, Neptune.*

47 *In one of the many, splendid coastal villas, where the rich inhabitants and merchants of Leptis withdrew after their city's port filled with sediment, this gorgeous mosaic portraying three characters was found. The villa was Dar Buch Ammara, near Zliten, located a few dozen miles east of Leptis. The mosaic, called "the four seasons," was removed from its original location and then moved to and reassembled at the Museum of the Castle in Tripoli. The three allegorical figures represent winter, with the rare tuft of grass; summer, wrapped in garlands of fruit; and autumn, who celebrates the reaping of the wheat. In the mosaic, beyond inevitable spring, the products and human activities corresponding to the four seasons are illustrated. The mosaic was marvelously crafted and completed with multicolored geometrical designs.*

The Urban Face of the Country

48 top *A monument dedicated to the fallen of the Libyan resistance to the Italian invasion is found at Misurata. Inside the structure, a small museum has been set up.*

48 bottom left *Zliten is a small city on the Libyan coast east of Tripoli. Among its buildings, the mosque dedicated to Sidi Abdusalam, a marabout to which numerous miracles have been attributed, stands out.*

48 bottom right *This airy building is found in Misurata, a well-cared-for city and home to some of the more well-known and shrewd Libyan businessmen.*

48-49 *From the archeological area of Leptis, the view extends over the modern buildings of Al-Khums, an industrial town where the main cement factory in the country is located.*

50-51 and 51 top Benghazi, is the second-largest city in Libya for number of inhabitants, but the citizens do not willing accept simple statistics. They proudly defend their cultural supremacy linked to ancient origins.

Benghazi and the borderlands of Cyrenaica have seen the expansion and establishment throughout the country of the Senussi religious group, to which King Idriss, who was overthrown by Gheddaffi's revolution, belonged.

51 center A line of bright-white buildings characterizes the panorama of the town of Derna, the jewel of Cyrenaica during the colonial era. Unfortunately, it has lost much of its charm.

51 bottom The aerial view of Tobruq makes it possible to observe the modern port and the recently built buildings. Nothing remains of the old city that was once the setting for numerous battles during the Second World War.

People between
the Sea and the Desert

52 top The whole population of Libya numbers around four and a half million inhabitants. Many immigrants, above all North Africans, are excluded from this figure. In recent years, the Libyan government has implemented a series of economic policies and cooperation agreements with many states throughout Africa to encourage the flow of students and workers.

52 bottom The Tuareg have always known the Sahara better than anyone; it is almost obligatory to trust oneself to one of them as a guide on tourist excursions. Despite modern satellite technology, exploring or hunting down important sites and caves with paintings or rock drawings becomes a difficult task without their help and profound knowledge of the desert's tricks.

53 An elderly man wears the typical head covering that protects from the winter cold. Many older Libyans attended school during the colonial government and, thanks to their natural inclination for languages, still speak Italian perfectly.

54 *The scarves that some Libyan women wear on their heads are ever more a personal choice rather than a family or cultural imposition. Whether or not to wear the scarf has more do with the image they wish to project to the world.*

55 *top left and right The handicraft industry is not particularly well-developed in Libya. Clothing, handmade objects, and even carpets come mostly from abroad and are resold in the* souqs. *The coppersmiths are ancient experts in the shaping of copper. With their ancient but costly technique, they hammer out the blows that create various kinds of containers.*

55 *bottom Anyone who visits the medina of a Libyan city for the first time remains impressed by the large number of gold shops. In fact, gold is used in the majority of ceremonies; it serves to pay homage to someone, but also to emphasize one's economic and social status.*

Living with the Desert

56-57 The Mediterranean climate, ideal for olive trees, has always favored the Libyan production of olives. Today, agriculture is in crisis, and olive oil is more easily bought from other countries, even those that share a border such as Tunisia, because of proceeds from the petroleum industry. The old olive presses have passed into disuse or are only used for an almost family-based homemade-style production.

57 left The oases are not only about palm trees, but also the cultivation of vegetables, onions, potatoes, and more. Irrigation from the ancient wells or modern drilling brings water to the surface that, for thousands of years, has remained hidden, thus sprinkling the vastly dominant yellow color of the desert with green patches.

57 top right The gold seller who passes his time sitting on the ground in the medina of Tripoli did not manage to completely hide his face in time from the indiscreet gaze of the photographer.

57 bottom right A well of water, linked to an underground spring, represents a fundamental point of reference for the peoples of the desert. Knowing the spots where water naturally comes to the surface or where aquifers lie just a few feet below ground is critical for those who have to or want to live in such an inhospitable climate.

Fragments of Arab Culture

58 *left and right Two youths from Ghadames are decked out to a tee to take part in the wedding of a friend or relative. Weddings are opportunities to present oneself to society, they are the runways on which the elders see and judge young people in order to give their potential consent to future marriages.*

58-59 *The musicians are the only men to be allowed into the female section of the ceremony. The parties of the bride and groom are strictly separated and open only to relatives and friends of the same sex. Here, women accompany the melody of the flute on drums, and then they will eat and dance all night long, radiant in their glittering clothes.*

The Nomads
of the Dunes

60-61 Old but resistant trucks getting ready to cross the desert, often traveling what seem like race tracks, are loaded to unbelievable levels. Sacks, bins, and tanks of water and gasoline hang from every side of the trailer like a drowning man clings to his only hope in order to not be swallowed up by the voracious sands.

61 top At times, a few clandestine emigrants trust their salvation to these trucks, along with the goods they carry. In fact, Libya is the African country with the highest per-capita income, and even though the distribution of wealth is not the most equal in the world, thanks to a policy that guarantees a basket of basic foods at a very low price, no one dies of hunger.

61 bottom left and right The Tuareg head covering and sun glasses are two fundamental accessories for desert guides. Many Tuareg have left their camels in their corrals and instead cross the dunes behind the wheel of powerful off-road vehicles.

62-63 To make a Tuareg head
covering it takes even up to 23 or 26
feet, and then a series of wrapping
movements, between the head and neck,
to protect from the sun and, above all,
from the wind and sand storms.

63 top The natural caves created by
erosion were the first shelters of
prehistoric man. They were also the
first canvases where man portrayed
elements from his environment,
engraved the forms of animals,
and left accounts of his existence
for whoever, today, is lucky enough
to come across them and be totally
amazed.

63 bottom A group of camels has been
duly loaded up for departure. This
animal, since time immemorial,
represents the ideal companion for
travel and transport across the Sahara.
Their temper, docility, and resistance
to thirst as well as the protein-rich
milk they produce has made them
an indispensable tool for the
desert nomads.

64 Even in areas where the sand reigns supreme, among the limitless dunes of the Erg of Ubari or in the Idahan of Murzuk, trunks of dry wood can be found with which to build a fire for the night, which serves for cooking, as a reference point for those who drift off, and as a heat source during the freezing winter nights.

65 top The guides that lead tourists along the tracks of the Sahara understand the worth the immensity of the silence, the boundless sandy horizons, and the night sky lit by thousands of stars have for Western visitors. For this reason, they make camp in places that favor unique experiences, smiling discreetly at the amazement it brings.

65 bottom The periods of waiting, decision-making, traveling, reflection, and task-fulfilling are what constitute one of the great differences between men from the West and men of the desert. Tuareg guides live in the desert; waiting is part of life and not unproductive empty space between one activity and another. It is time to think and meditate.

Embraced by Sea and Sand

66 top In the middle of the Fezzan, the Ramla Douada is known as the zone of sand and lakes. More than 20 pools of water, with a difficult-to-classify geological origin, spring up, surrounded by palm and tamarisk trees. Some, like this one, dry up for periods during the year, or even forever, leaving behind a crust of pure salt over pebbles.

66 bottom This enchanting inlet at the Roman villa is called "Villa Silin". Besides taking pleasure in the building's floors covered by gorgeous mosaics, its private baths, and its small commercial port, its ancient owners could also enjoy the fine white sand and the transparent waters of the sea as could few others.

67 As the sun drops from its noontime height and slips sideways between the dunes, the light and shadows stand out, chasing each other, filling and emptying one's gaze, drawing thousands of soft shapes in perpetual movement. Perhaps this characteristic is part of the reason why the region has been called a "sea of sand." The sun moves the dunes as if they were the waves of the Mediterranean.

The Desert Alive

68-69 The highest temperature in all the country has been registered in the area of Tarhuna. Nonetheless, a river flows here year-round, feeding the oasis, although in recent years it has become ever drier. At its source, the small waterway forms a little waterfall that is onomatopoeiacally called "Sharshara," recalling the flow of water so rare in these parts.

69 top The Italian colonization of the country invested highly in agriculture and encouraging the intensive exploitation of the territory. Thousands of colonists, mostly from the south of Italy, were invited to leave their land for "Libya felix." A land concession, consisting of a certain number of acres, a fully equipped house, and a lot of hard work awaited them.

69 center In the pre-desert zone, it is not hard to come across structures dating back to Roman times. In general, they are fortresses that marked the southern limes *(the fortified frontier of the Roman Empire) or, as in this case, funereal monuments. In fact, the tombs were built outside towns, and the most important and sturdy ones have resisted time and numerous devastating invasions.*

69 bottom When the desert wrinkles and the rocks lift up forming rises, thanks to the magic of some water god, a spring of water flows through the fissures, as palm and eucalyptus trees seize the opportunity, marking the route of the underwater river with their green canopies. The spot becomes a rest area where men and animals can cool off.

70 top However, the quality of the water may be, it is still water, and even if the muddy color of this pond is not inviting, the presence of the vital liquid must still be appreciated. Knowing how to deal with scarce water resources is a trait of the people of the desert, who have built a culture around this fact of life.

70 center The white walls protect the inhabitants of a small village in the desert. The community living there is actually one big family that has come together and stuck together because of the difficult environment. Occasions for group events are many, but there is also time for a solitary stroll as the sun weakens in the evening.

70 bottom The cool closeness of a simple mosque inspires concentration and prayer, as the sound of silence is broken only by the call of the muezzin *who, five times a day according to the prescribed hours of prayer, summons the faithful.*

70-71 Those who mixed, with their bare hands, the mortar for the inside and outside walls of this Saharan village also shaped the domes of the mosques and the typical barbs that, sticking out from corners and angles, unequivocally characterize the towns of Fezzan. Such a particular feature has even remained part of the designs for new buildings.

72-73 In Ghat, contrasts are obvious: the old city of the desert, centralized in a single gathering of walls and alleys, of roofs and terraces, all in earth tones, sits next to, as if in respect for the hard work of the older builders, the new, white buildings among which are found, as always and everywhere, the mosque with its minaret.

73 left The photograph shows a detail of one of the fortified granaries built by the Berbers, a population that, upon the arrival of the Arabs, withdrew to the mountains of the Tripoli Jebel, retaining only one outlet on the sea near Zuara, the Libyan city where, apart from Arabic, a dialect of Berber origin is still spoken.

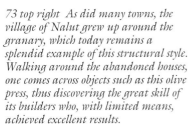

73 top right As did many towns, the village of Nalut grew up around the granary, which today remains a splendid example of this structural style. Walking around the abandoned houses, one comes across objects such as this olive press, thus discovering the great skill of its builders who, with limited means, achieved excellent results.

73 center right The fortified granary, with a circular section, contained thousands of small cells in which the provisions of every family were stored.

73 bottom right The simplicity of the earliest mosques reflects the origins of Islam. Already at the time, the themes of Muslim religious architecture were being defined, such as the use of arches and vaults, the orientation towards Mecca, the absence of paintings on the walls, and a cozy atmosphere.

Atmosphere in Blue and Ochre

74 top It is not true that the dunes move swiftly; only the surface level of fine dust actually shifts. Their form stays unaltered, at least over the span of a human lifetime. However, underfoot, the continuous swirling of sand particles makes the body and mind sway.

74 bottom It does not matter what is the precise place where the photographer was enchanted by the sinuosity of this dune; the sky and the waves designed by the wind could be found at any point in the Sahara. The desert rejects the geography of longitudes and latitudes for another system tied more to colors, shapes, and silence.

74-75 To reach some areas of the Akakus, it is necessary to be familiar with its many passes. Understanding and respecting the environment without violating it, but rather complying with its openings, must be the way with which one undertakes a journey in this region, where the rocks and sand play at creating idyllic places as well as invisible dangers.

76-77 In the distance, one of the rocky formations sticking out of the area of the Tadrart Akakus is visible, while the big sand dune in the foreground displays its typical wind-drawn ripples.

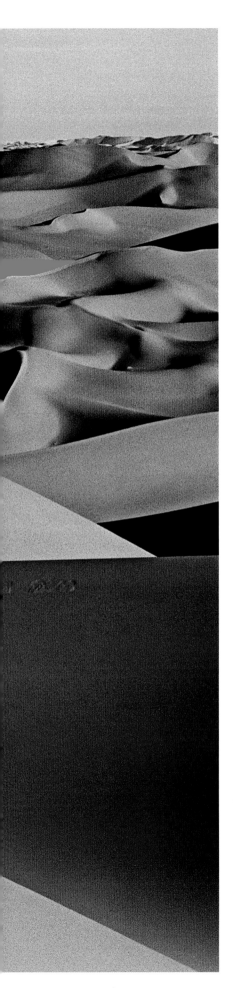

78-79 The photo reveals the extremely tall and little known dunes of Idahan in Murzuk, a sandy region south of the Valley of Life (Wadi el-Hayat), in the southern area of Fezzan. The first Western explorer to visit it appears to have been Ardito Desio, during the 1930s.

79 top The Ramla Douada takes its name from the ancient inhabitants that lived on the shores of the lakes sprinkled throughout the region. The population of the Douada lived off "worms" and "worm eaters," as other peoples of the desert defined them. In reality, this referred to the tiny crustaceans that lived in the salt water, which must have had a high caloric and nutritional content considering that they constituted the base of the local diet.

79 center The waters of the lake of Gabroun are as still as a mirror, and the image of the dunes is perfectly reflected. They are also highly salty waters, as one realizes upon entering the water because of how well one floats.

79 bottom To move among the tall dunes of the Murzuk Desert, one must know the area well. Because few visitors come to the region, the wind quickly erases any tracks before they can settle.

80-81 From the top of a dune, one of the lakes of the Ramla Douada appears in all its glory. The surrounding palm trees and vegetation make for a pleasant place to stop.

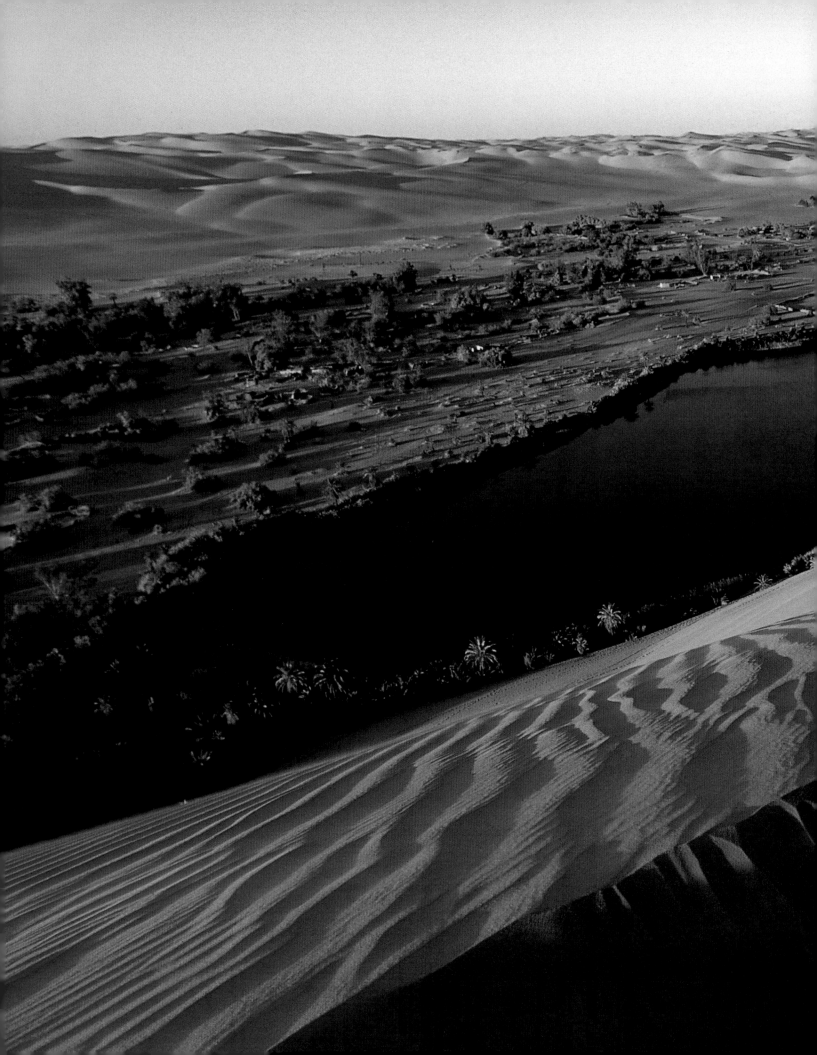

82-83 One of the more famous rock paintings of the Fezzan portrays the Garamantes population. Little is known of their culture beyond that garnered from the accounts of ancient historians, but from this and other images it has been deduced that they were formidable charioteers and that they drove around the desert on very light chariots pulled by two or four horses.

83 top The Saharan civilization, which left behind its rock drawings and paintings, reached the height of their development between 10,000 and 5,000 B.C. The places where illustrations with historical as well as artistic value are still discovered today are the natural caves and shelters among the cliffs of the Tadrart Akakus Mountain chain.

83 center When possible, a method largely used by archeologists, known as "Carbon 14," exists for dating finds. It calculates the radioactive residue contained in substances present in living beings. Unfortunately, the method is not applicable to inorganic objects, such as rock objects and drawings.

83 bottom *The method for preparing colors, with which the drawings on rock walls were filled in, consisted in crushing pieces of clay, other stones, or animal or plant residues. Mixing them with water made it possible to create a color that, in most cases, has proven to be quite long lasting.*

Akakus:
An Open-air Museum

84 top Up until just a few decades ago when archeological interest in the area was raised, the Akakus region had remained unexplored, apart from the occasional Tuareg hunting expedition. In effect, thanks to their tall and steep rock walls, the two massifs of Tadrart and Akakus, of similar geological formation, have guarded the area from the simply "curious" for years.

84 center Fabrizio Mori was the first archeologist-explorer to penetrate beyond the rocky walls, thanks to the help of camels, and discover the first works in this "open-air museum." In later years, a track was opened that could be driven even by off-road vehicles, the so-called "Mori Track," still used today by the majority of visitors.

84 bottom The Akakus, heavily traveled in Neolithic times, can be considered a "desert" in the deepest etymological sense of the word: an "abandoned" place, a space defined by having been something in the past of which only traces, ruins, and echoes remain in the present.

84-85 The hot and dry air that is breathed by day among the rocks of the Akakus, as in the majority of the Sahara, is like a cure-all for the body. The lack of humidity makes it possible to withstand the air even very high temperatures. The surprise, however, comes on winter nights, when an icy frost covers the sand. It is a good idea to protect oneself very well before sleeping.

86 left The deep valleys that cross the whole territory of the Sahara were once rivers, often even with strong currents. The beds of these waterways, now dry, are called wadi.

86 right The clouds drifting fast and high above must not mislead one to think it might rain. Over the course of the year, the days when the sky magnanimously offers a few

sprinkles of water can be counted on one's hand, if at all in some years.

87 The hustle and bustle of ancient times on the sea and on prehistoric waterways, the smoothing action of the strong winds that sweep the sands and shape the mountains, the various resistance levels of the different types of rock: all this hard

work over time is written on the plunging walls of the Tadrart Akakus massif, imprinted in indelible letters.

88-89 The horizon, immense and curved, does not reveal anything else but sand and sand yet again. The mind cannot avoid dealing with this infinite dimension in this uniform setting.

Window on the Mediterranean

90 top and bottom The earth's crust that slips into the blue sea of the Cyrenaica, thanks to the jagged form of the coastline, offers excellent protection to the fish life. The grouper, which fishermen and scuba-diving tourists have such difficulty encountering in the rest of the Mediterranean, can be seen here even from the shoreline, as they swim peacefully just under the surface of the water.

91 The Cyrenaic Sea communicates with the sandstone, as does the rest of the Libyan coast, but it also converses with the rocks of the Green Mountain that, particularly in the Marmarica region, reach far enough down to be lapped by the last of the waves. The result is a combination of Liguria and Sardinia, the Greece of the Cyclades and the Turkish coast. It is the highest expression of what the Mediterranean Sea is all about.

92-93 *Tolmeita is the modern town that has been built up a few steps away from the archeological site of ancient Ptolemais. For its few inhabitants, life here proceeds in ignorance of the magnificent past of their land.*

93 top *The low rocks tenderly embrace the sea. A natural landing point, like numerous others along the coastline in the area of Apollonia, explains why the Greeks from Santorini Island chose this part of the Mediterranean to set up colonies.*

93 bottom *In the area of Leptis Magna, low bushes typical of the Mediterranean flora sprout and grow on the sand that reaches the sea.*

94-95 *The zone of Apollonia was the ideal landing spot for the numerous crafts that carried goods to and from Cyrene.*

96-97 *The enormous foot of a giant Cyclops extends a toe into the sea at Tobruk. The inhabitants of this region farm the mountain terraces or the strip of coastal plain.*

Traces of the Past

98 top At the end of the Severian Forum, the heart of imperial Leptis, one of the most particular and beautiful buildings of the entire archeological district is found: the basilica. Besides the columns that divide the nave from the aisles, on the two short sides of the rectangular layout, four square-based columns sculpted completely with floral motifs and depictions of the labors of Hercules are found.

98 bottom Jason Magnus was a very well-known priest of the temple of Apollo in Cyrene. His house is the most luxurious in the whole city. The headless statues that stand out in the photo delimit one of the sides of the large house inside which extraordinary floor mosaics can be admired.

99 The large street that crossed this quarter of Sabratha is still perfectly serviceable. The sophisticated technique used to place the blocks has maintained it in working condition for thousands of years.

Sabratha: From Phoenician Emporium to Roman Colony

100-101 The large size of the columns of the temple of Liber Pater in Sabratha attest to the importance given to this divinity, worshiped throughout North Africa in the past. The temple dates back to the second century A.D., the great period in the history of the three cities on the Cyrenaic coast: Sabratha, Oea, and Leptis Magna.

101 top Besides recalling the Antonine Dynasty, which also included Marcus Aurelius and Lucius Verus, this temple, whose construction dates back to the first century A.D., grants one of the broadest views over the whole archeological area of Sabratha thanks to its stairway and raised terrace – yet further reasons why it is one of the more well-visited.

101 bottom How many columns arrived from around the known world and how many were built across the Libyan territory over the years! The archeological areas were, for centuries, outdoor warehouses for whomever needed pillars for constructions of all kinds, many of which have remained upright or are still lying on the ground awaiting use.

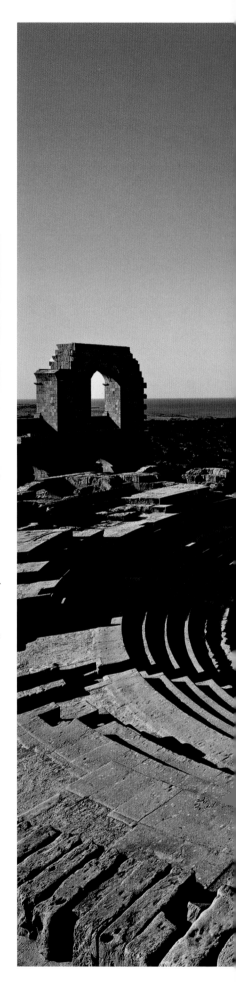

102 top left The amphitheater of Sabratha could seat about 5,000 spectators, thus guaranteeing it first place among the theaters of Roman North Africa. Built at the end of the second century A.D., the splendid white-marble and black-granite columns create a powerful chromatic effect.

102 bottom left Close to the sea, slightly on the outskirts of the city's central neighborhoods, the structure of the amphitheater stands with its scene featuring three orders of columns reaching 82 feet tall. Its present-day appearance is due to the efforts of Italo Balbo, governor of Libya, who made it an important symbol of the ancient Roman presence in the country.

102 right The shapes of numerous characters from Greek and Roman mythology discreetly emerge from the duly restored pulpit of the theater. The gorgeous group of the Three Graces, an extremely refined example of sculptural skill, can be seen here.

103 The stage of the Sabratha amphitheater, reconstructed with wooden boards, still hosts a series of various types of shows today. They take place around sunset, when the sun melts like liquid into the sea and the clouds blush with the tired light.

*104 top Many of the lovely mosaics
found on the floors of the houses,
baths, and the other buildings of
Sabratha are displayed at the Roman
museum on the perimeter of the
archeological area.*

*104 bottom As usual in Roman cities,
the amphitheater stood outside the
walls. The heavy flow of spectators, the
special nature of the shows held there,
and the presence of ferocious animals
made this position highly advisable.*

*105 The magnificence and authority
of Jupiter undeniably emanates from
this bust held at the Museum of
Sabratha. The rendering of his long
hair and beard leaves no doubt about
the skill of the sculptors of the era and
endows the father of the gods with a
natural look.*

Leptis Magna: The Homeland of the Severus Dynasty

106-107 The amphitheater of Leptis remains, in its dignified decadence, a "spectacular" place.

107 top Septimius Severus wanted his birthplace to be one of the most beautiful in the Mediterranean and had it paved with the most precious kinds of marble. The arch that gives access to the city is dedicated to him.

107 bottom The first phase of construction on the amphitheater of Leptis Magna dates back to the first century A.D.

108-109 The view from above emphasizes the areas of Leptis in which the restoration projects have been the most incisive.

110 top The Gorgons watch over visitors to the Forum of the Severii from the high-up pediments of the colonnades. Some are still in their original position, whereas others await placement on the ground or stare languidly at visitors in archeological museums.

110 center On the main cardi and decumani of Roman cities – streets that divided neighborhoods into regular blocks – arches dedicated to important people often rise. Near the market and theater, the arches of Tiberius and Trajan are still standing.

110 bottom Without a good guide, it is quite difficult to identify the numerous buildings in the Old Forum of Leptis. It is necessary to keep in mind the overlapping of epochs in which materials were re-used and the area was re-organized until it was finally abandoned following the building of the newer Severian Forum.

110-111 The construction of the market of Leptis, near the area where the theater would soon stand, was completed in the early years of the first century A.D. thanks to the sponsorship of one Annobal Rufus. Originally, it was one of the most artistically special places in the city.

112 *The large stones of the theater's steps turn red at sunset, the calm sea amplifies the silence, the tufts of grass expand between the seats, and the columns of the temples look ceaselessly towards the sky as the new show, composed of missing sounds, invisible actors, memories, and imagination, begins.*

113 left *Villa Silin is an open-air museum: some of the most sophisticated mosaics from the illustrious past of the Libyan coast remain where they were installed by their first owners. It seems that the most refined and centrally located portions, made using the smallest-size* tesserae, *arrived pre-assembled by far away artist-artisans and that, on site, only the peripheral parts of the design were mounted.*

113 top right *Two hunters tracking a wild animal characterize this wall painting from the Hunting Baths, on the outskirts of the city. The thermal rooms were roofed with newly built domes to protect their ornate iconographic decoration.*

113 center right *The stone blocks, piled on the edge of the sea, were part of Leptis Magna's port. They became redundant when the course of the Libda River deviated, the barriers of the port extended towards the sea, and the current that washed out the sand was blocked.*

113 bottom right *The peristyle in Villa Silin probably had a beautiful pool embellished with mosaics. However, the view of the sea from this splendid terrace is still today sweet and soothing.*

Ptolemais:
A Hellenistic Inheritance

114 top The small Museum of
Ptolemais contains some
extraordinary pieces found during
excavations of the archeological area,
among them the extremely well-made
mosaics found in the palace called "of
the columns."

114 center left In the Byzantine era,
the governor of the city and the
surrounding areas was called dux.
He administered justice and lived in
a palace that looked like a fortified
building, divided cleanly into two
zones for two distinct purposes.

114 center right A tour of the ruins
of Ptolemais is an experience that
even those not overly enthusiastic
about archeology can appreciate.

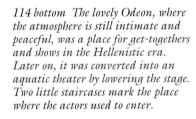

114 bottom The lovely Odeon, where
the atmosphere is still intimate and
peaceful, was a place for get-togethers
and shows in the Hellenistic era.
Later on, it was converted into an
aquatic theater by lowering the stage.
Two little staircases mark the place
where the actors used to enter.

114-115 By far the most important
and extravagant building in
Ptolemais is the Palace of the
Columns, which covers an area of
over 64,000 square feet.

Apollonia: The Port of Cyrene

116-117 In the Byzantine era, the columns of the pagan temples of Apollonia were re-used to support the ceilings and divide the nave from the aisles in basilicas. Walking east within a few feet of the sea, three basilicas in a row are encountered, respectively called western, central, and eastern.

117 left Throughout the Mediterranean, the Byzantines spread the message of Christ and all of its symbolic devices along with it. Moreover, even though they re-used, for obvious reasons, the materials that they found of Greek and Roman origin, they adapted the few small details to suit their needs.

117 right In the three photos, the Byzantine basilicas of Apollonia are shown. Along the Cyrenaic coast, similar buildings can be found as well as others that still await exploration. They all have the same structure; in some cases the typical mosaic floors have remained on site, in others they have been lifted and moved elsewhere. The basilicas were also built outside the towns to make the religious structures accessible not only to the urban population but also to the farmers and country folk.

118-119 The lonely palm tree, grown spontaneously on the stage of the small theater of Apollonia, seems to have an affection for this space, once upon a time much livelier.

117

Cyrene:
The Athens of Africa

120 top and center left The two photos capture, from two different angles, the area that was first colonized by the earliest inhabitants of Cyrene: the vast terrace on which stands the sanctuary of Apollo. The colonists from Santorini Island had turned to this god for advice about where they should settle their new city.

120 bottom In Roman times, the Greek theater was converted into an amphitheater where the cries of gladiators, lions, and the audience clashed with the atmosphere of the sacred place on the outskirts of town. For this reason, a wide and prudish wall was built to separate the sacred from the profane.

120 center right The Doric columns of the Greek propylaea of Cyrene stand out on the dome in contrast with the sky and surrounded by dense vegetation. Tons of tourists crowd in to visit one of the most interesting sites in the whole Mediterranean and enjoy the vestiges of its luminous past.

120-121 The sanctuary of Apollo covers a natural shelf on the northern slopes of the Acropolis. The temple dedicated to the main Cyrenaic divinity, as it appears today, is actually the result of a series of construction projects that followed one another over the course of the centuries beginning with the original structure from an ancient era.

122 top Traveling the street that originally ran alongside the track where the athletes trained is spectacular. The figures of a beardless Hermes and a thick-bearded Hercules oversee and protect passers-by, leaning out from the short columns holding them up. At a later date, the street was covered and became a path between the new forum and the agora.

122 center left In every Greek city, the agora was the hub of public life. That of Cyrene remained the focal point until the Roman conquest, which transferred the heart of civic relations to the new forum, built on the prior site of the gymnasium.

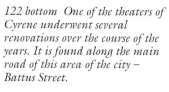

122 bottom One of the theaters of Cyrene underwent several renovations over the course of the years. It is found along the main road of this area of the city – Battus Street.

122 center right The strong and bearded Heracles materializes out of one of the columns along Battus Street. His celebrated 12 labors were well suited to being portrayed on porticoes, columns, and capitals.

122-123 The young citizens and the soldiers of Cyrene used the wide spaces of the Ptolemaion for exercising and combat practice. The building, which dates back to the second century B.C., was probably the work of Ptolemy VIII.

124 *In the agora stands the naval monument, erected between the second and third centuries B.C. following a sea victory. For a figurehead, it features a statue of Nike, the winged victor (unfortunately missing her wings and head), on the starboard bow.*

125 top *A ritualistic women's procession, commemorated by the great Greek poet Kallimachus in one of his hymns, began at this circular-shaped temple. The two statues portraying Demeter, goddess of fertility, and her daughter Koré (Persephone), goddess of the underworld, are well recognizable. Small drainage canals suggest that the place was the site of animal sacrifices.*

125 center *This prized marble gateway is all that remains of the façade of the temple of Apollo Archegetes, which stood on the west side of the agora. An inscription found on site documents its dedication to this divinity.*

125 bottom *The temple "of the Hexagon Foundations" dates back to the second century B.C. and was laid out on the spot were a building used to stand dedicated to Aristeus, a founding divinity of the medicine of Cyrene, whose cult continued to worship in the new temple structure.*

Ghirza: The Monumental Necropolises

126 The road leading to the monumental area of Ghirza is the path beaten by the installation of the big pipes connected with the "Great River" project. This feat of engineering has made it possible for many visitors to explore one of the most interesting archeological areas in the country.

126-127 The features of the monumental tombs of Ghirza are a combination of the Roman model and elements from the Saharan culture.

128 Uprighting the stump of a sandstone Doric column and placing it upon a well-decorated capital, also in sandstone, is enough to restore dignity and purpose to the vestiges of a past packed with art and history.